W9-BFN-659

Heartbeats: The Izzat Project

WRITTEN BY THE IZZAT COLLECTIVE
Aruba A., Kulsoom Ahmad, Kathana Ratnakara, M. Ahmad, Nadia Alam, S.B., AND Siva, WITH Farrah Khan AND Roxanna Vahed

ILLUSTRATED BY
Somya Singh WITH Selena Wong

POMEGRANATE TREE GROUP PRESS 2012, 2014
SECOND EDITION

Pomegranate Tree Group

Heartbeats: The IZZAT Project

©Pomegranate Tree Group Press 2012, 2014
Second Edition

All rights reserved. No part of this book may be reproduced or transmitted in any form without written permission from the publisher, except by reviewers who may quote brief excerpts in connection with a review.

ISBN 978-0-9917936-0-0

www.pomegranatetreegroup.ca

PEER COORDINATORS
M. Ahmad & Kathana Ratnakara

PROJECT COORDINATOR & THERAPIST
Farrah Khan

EXPRESSIVE ARTS THERAPIST & DRAMATURGE
Roxanna Vahed

PROJECT ADVISORS
Deepa Mattoo and Mandeep Kaur Mucina

BOOK DESIGNER
Kashfia Rahman

COVER ILLUSTRATION
Somya Singh

EDITORS
Jamila-Khanom Allidina and Farrah Khan

This special edition of Heartbeats was generously funded by

Thank you to the gracious funders of our initial project

TABLE OF CONTENTS

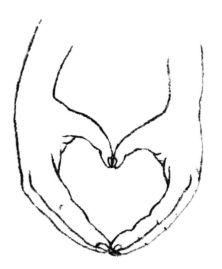

Pomegranate Tree Group

Pomegranate Tree Group (PTG) is a organization that works to support diverse communities' resiliencies through critical conscious raising, research and consulting. Our approach is rooted in cultivating seeds of possibility, maintaining critical connections, and fostering transformative engagement in communities.

BEGINNINGS

Heartbeats: The IZZAT Project is an expressive arts project in which young South Asian women use illustration, writing and theatre to explore and share community stories about resilience in the face of violence.

THE IZZAT GROUP

In the late fall of 2011, the Pomegranate Tree Group, with the support of the Barbra Schlifer Commemorative Clinic, worked with a peer coordinator to form the *IZZAT Project* group. Seven young South Asian women came together from March to September of 2012 to share stories, heal, and participate in arts-based workshops.

CREATIVE PROCESS

The stories we shared during our sessions were garnered through conversations with our peers, community members, novels, and various news sources. *IZZAT Project* group members developed these conversations into six stories. We read drafts out loud and, through role playing and other theatre games, drew out the key parts of our stories. We met numerous times as a group and were individually mentored by editors to further refine the stories. The illustrations were created from our sketches, discussions and continuous feedback. The final product is *Heartbeats: The IZZAT Project.*

INTRODUCTION

DEAR READERS,

Remember these two things...

We are doing this out of love.
Our lives have changed since we wrote these stories, because...
>   ...we got older.
>   ...we fought back.

We are trying to find safety even as you read these words...
>   Because we have had new experiences.
>   Because we have met new people.
>   Because our relationships to these stories have changed.
>   Because it was a form of release.
>   Because we had to move back home, against our will.
>   Because we negotiated.
>   Because we have new things to look forward to.
>   Because we met each other...

We, the authors of these stories are
>   Young South Asian Women.
>   Visionaries. Healers. Storytellers...

>   ...We are more than words can describe.

We have a lot to say:

We have a complicated relationship to our families.

Mother Father Sister Brother Auntie Uncle Cousin...

...On some of the harder days, it seems like all we hear is:

Think about our reputation
Don't be selfish
What will so-and-so think?
Good girls don't
Proper girls should
Pray on time!
You're so lazy
Your lipstick is too bright
Your clothes are too tight
So-and-so's daughter is obedient
You have no shame!
Such a bad daughter!

To our families:

...We wrote these stories out of love.

DEAR MOM AND DAD,

We love you.

These stories are drawn from our peers' and our own experiences. Don't second guess, or tell us we're being "dramatic." Please try to relate and understand. Also, can you stop caring about what other people think?

More than anything we want unconditional love. We want support, hope, happiness, and to have a say in our future.

If we moved out, we want you to understand how hard and painful it was for us to make that decision.

And not all of us can or even always feel we have to leave. This doesn't mean we aren't hurting, or struggling to find a better way to be with you. We want to feel good with our family.

With Hope

DEAR SISTER AND BROTHER,

Thank you for supporting us.
We understand you were hurt when you said those things.
You are so important to us.
Even with the distance we think of you.
We miss you.
We wish you would try to understand our perspective.
You have helped us find our courage.
We were angry and hurt when you stopped talking to us.
We want you in our lives.
We can't see you if you're going to treat us that way.

We will always love you.

To those people who are supposed to help- teachers, social workers, health care providers etc.:

If I come to you for support:

I need someone that I can trust and that will LISTEN to me. Listen to what I'm saying. Acknowledge my feelings. Admit that you don't know. And don't say you understand.

Oh, and know that I DON'T need your pity, or assumptions. I do need comfort and support. I need you to say you believe that this is happening. That what I'm telling you is important, and real, that it's serious, and that you believe me. And that it's not my fault. And I need you to understand that sometimes my concerns need to be dealt with right away.

Remember that I'm an individual. Ask me what I want. And ask me or help me clarify what I need and what I think is best for me. What will feel safest? Sometimes that might mean staying in my community, and sometimes that might mean figuring out how to leave. But, listen to ME.

We have two more things to say—to the media, and to our larger communities.

To the media:

We are listening.

We hear you when you shape your story around the idea that there is something inherently wrong with our culture. We hear you when you wrap your racism in a cultural cloak. We hear you when you insinuate that we, as South Asian women, are "asking for it" because we are connected to our communities.

Hear us: South Asian communities and cultures are not static. We know that violence is happening, just like in other communities. Know this: our communities and cultures have also been sites of resistance, safety, and joy for us.

We get it: calling family violence "honour" crimes creates more drama, sells more papers, gets higher network ratings, but it also excuses the general Canadian public.

What is it with making it seem like gender-based violence doesn't happen in families that are white, middle-class, perhaps Christian— or whatever you think "normal" means these days? When was that ever true?

You make it harder for us to have conversations about violence in our homes when we have to deal with all the racism or ignorance that your reporting is soaked in.

It silences us and our communities.
It pushes away engagement.
It's exhausting.

You know what? We experience many kinds of violence: racism, homophobia, bullying, poverty etc. But we also experience pride, support, love and acceptance. Can you talk about that too?

We believe that the violence will end. And that you, the media, can play a big role in that.

Start seeing how WE shape our lives.
Stop speaking on our behalf.
Don't perpetuate stereotypes.
Stop generalizing us.
Stop trying to save us.
Support us.
Make way when we claim space to share our stories.
Amplify our voices.

And finally, to our diverse, complicated, vibrant, funny, fluid communities:

We are not alone in this—violence is happening in every community.

Naming violence can feel like airing dirty community laundry and this is not our intention. We know that ending the cycle of violence makes us good people, daughters, granddaughters, sisters, cousins, nieces, friends, community members.

Please know that when we disagree, calling us "white" or accusing us of acting like "those people" won't make our ideas go away, and it dishonours the history of resistance that many of our ancestors have come from.

Sometimes it feels like you fear anything that is different…

And yes, we know there are good things to talk about—but right now there are some difficult things we aren't talking about, namely family violence. It is hurting us, putting some of our lives—the lives of siblings, elders, children—in danger.

When violence happens in our families, we need a different response… not stigma, shame or guilt, but support, understanding and a commitment to change things.

We know that many of us, if not all of us, are survivors of violence, be it physical assault, colonization, racism, sexism, partition, or forced marriage. We believe that our communities can be sites of healing.

To survivors, we are healing together and individually. Thank you for being.

*We are young South Asian women who have seen, felt, heard
violence in our homes, our communities, and the world outside.*

We are
compassionate
brave
courageous
committed to being ourselves without fear
hilarious
good listeners
artists
committed to honouring ourselves

we are
beautiful
outspoken
tough
fierce

And we are sharing these stories with you
    Sister
    Mother
    Brother
    Father
    Family

Friends
    Community

Because
We deserve
To Heal
Be heard
Reach out
Feel safe
love

     love
     love
     love

love

With love

THE IZZAT PROJECT

FOREWORD

DEAR PARENTS,

Every daughter knows her mother's heartbeat. She learns it, as do sons, snuggled in the womb. As parents, it becomes our job, our Heartbeats Project, to listen to hers. In this book, our daughters' heartbeats ask you for unconditional love and to admire their beauty; their fierceness; their passions and talents; their voices; their politics; their fun; their queer and straight identities.

They also ask you to reject their marriageability. I am an immigrant mother who has worked in the field of domestic violence for over thirty years. Twelve years ago, a 16-year-old Indian girl called me, desperate that her parents' plans for a forced marriage left her no choice but to run away from home. I asked her to wait until I figured out some way to help her, but it was too late. Neither of us could stop what her parents, grandparents, aunties, and uncles were determined to do. So I started learning about forced marriage and about strategies to be supportive, to stop the practice, and to criticize our culture for growing mothers and fathers who pressure, push, and damage our daughters. My teachers were teenage girls and young women like Kathana, Aruba, Kulsoom, M., Nadia, S.B., Siva, Somya, Selena, Roxanna and Farrah – the authors, illustrators, and organizers of the Izzat Collective.

Our daughters' book brings South Asian parents, families, communities, and activists a wonderful gift: the gift of re-imagining izzat, of new cultural meanings for an old concept that has brought suffering, family violence, intolerance, revenge, and an absurd preoccupation with what others will think of us if we don't suppress our daughters' freedoms.

Why is this the world we offer our daughters? Why do we think that betraying the trust they put in their mother's heartbeats and their father's love is the best thing for them? Why do we believe in a culture of izzat that allows us to crush a daughter's spirit and justify it as honorable duty?

Last year, I was unable to stop the forced departure of a college student carrying a heart full of fear, surrounded by ten izzat-driven relatives on a plane. A few days before the wedding, she killed herself. I couldn't have stopped that. But her mother and father, her aunties and uncles, and her grandparents could have if they had listened to what she wanted. This is not a story about a young woman being "dramatic" or selfish, or about blaming her parents for her death – this is the story our daughters are telling us in their book; their love letter to all of us: "Listen to us about what we want for our lives."

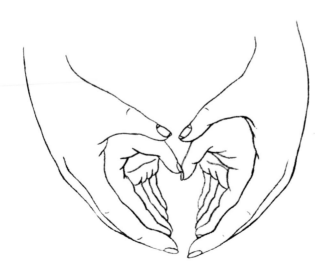

To them, pride in family, community and culture is about using our collective South Asian power to define culture instead of letting it define us. After all, both individual and cultural DNA changes with every generation. When our daughters see cultures of violence, homophobia and coercive control against women and girls, they see a cycle of shame. And how dare we justify that as protecting izzat?

Our story-tellers have given us a new meaning of izzat: freedom to be a bike messenger, join a graffiti project, fall in love with a woman; resistance to being the 'good daughter', to being stereotyped for wearing a hijab; strength to find their own path even if it involves the pain of leaving home, to heal, to thrive; and most of all, love – be it unconditional love for family or for the very communities and cultures that oppress them.

They take pride in all of you, and they ask that you be proud of them.

Like the pomegranate tree in the story that weeps at being uprooted and disdained and yet generously sustains life and grows new roots, our daughters have shown us their heartbeats. I am deeply inspired by the powerful heartbeats of Izzat they offer us. I hope you will be too.

Sincerely,

FIROZA CHIC DABBY

Firoza Chic Dabby is the Director of the Asian & Pacific Islander Institute on Domestic Violence, a national resource center in San Francisco, California. Our vision of gender democracy drives our mission to strengthen advocacy, change systems, and prevent gender violence through community transformation.

We hope that these stories will bring about dialogue and discussion.

We recognize that they may have an impact on you, the reader.

You are invited to do whatever makes you feel grounded
and cared for as you go through this book.

Open your heart:

listen to its rhythm

Breathe.

Breathe in love, support, compassion;

Breathe out;

Breathe in strength, resiliency, wisdom;

Breathe out.

Breathe in.

Breathe out.

THE BAD DAUGHTER

AUNTIE G

A GOOD DAUGHTER LOOKS LIKE THIS:

IS RELIGIOUS AND WILL WEAR WHAT WE WANT HER TO;

PURSUES A CAREER IN LAW, SCIENCE OR ENGINEERING;

AND SHE IS MARRIED AT 25 YEARS OLD.

UNCLE G

A BAD DAUGHTER LOOKS LIKE THIS:

LEAVES HER HAIR NATURAL SO SHE LOOKS LIKE A JONGLI;

GETTING CLOSER TO SHOWING SOME CLEAVAGE... UH-OH!

AND SHE ISN'T THINKING ABOUT MARRIAGE, POSSIBLY LEADING HER TO BE UNWED EVEN AT AGE 30!!

WRITTEN BY : NADIA ALAM
DRAWN BY : SOMYA SINGH

IN THE CASE OF THE HAQUES, THEIR DAUGHTER BECAME BAD WHEN SHE HAD THE NERVE TO ACTUALLY MOVE OUT FROM HER PARENT'S PLACE.*

OUT OF SERVICE

I'M MOVING OUT
I'M MOVING OUT
I'M MOVING OUT

* - EVEN THOUGH SHE TOLD THEM SHE WOULD, 3 TIMES!!!

THIS DAUGHTER WAS SO **BAD** THAT SHE HAD THE AUDACITY TO GET A JOB, STARTED BUYING HER OWN FURNITURE AND PAINTING HER NEW PLACE AS IF IT WERE HER "HOME." SHE WOULDN'T EVEN PICK UP THE PHONE WHEN HER FATHER CALLED.

THE **BAD** DAUGHTER THEN DARED TO START MAKING FOOD FOR HERSELF WITHOUT DEPENDING ON THE HOMEMADE CURRIES MADE BY HER MOM, WHICH WERE ALWAYS READY TO EAT AFTER SCHOOL OR WORK. WHAT KIND OF FOOD IS THIS ANYWAY? IT IS LIKE EATING GRASS...

THE **BAD** DAUGHTER STARTED REALIZING SHE COULD FINALLY PURSUE HER PASSION FOR THE ARTS AND NO LONGER SUPPRESS HER TALENTS, WITHOUT UNDERSTANDING HOW MUCH THIS WILL AFFECT HER MARRIAGEABILITY!

THE **BAD** DAUGHTER WAS EXPLORING MANY FAITHS IN HOPES OF BEING COMFORTABLE WITH ONE THAT SHE COULD CHOOSE FOR HERSELF, AND IN THE PROCESS, SHE BECAME A **BAD** MUSLIM TOO.

ASTAGFIRULLAH!

TSK! TSK!

OM

QU'RAN

THE <u>BAD</u> DAUGHTER STARTED DOING ALL THE <u>THINGS</u> SHE THOUGHT SHE NEVER COULD... SHE BECAME A SKILLED DOWNTOWN BIKER...

... SHE PARTIED AND HAD FUN (SHE'LL GO TO HELL FOR THIS OF COURSE)... AND INVITED GIRLS <u>AND</u> BOYS OVER TO HER PLACE.

DING DONG

IN SHORT, WE BOTH AGREED, KALPANA BECAME A WHITE PERSON! HER POOR, POOR PARENTS.

YOU DON'T KNOW ME AT ALL!!

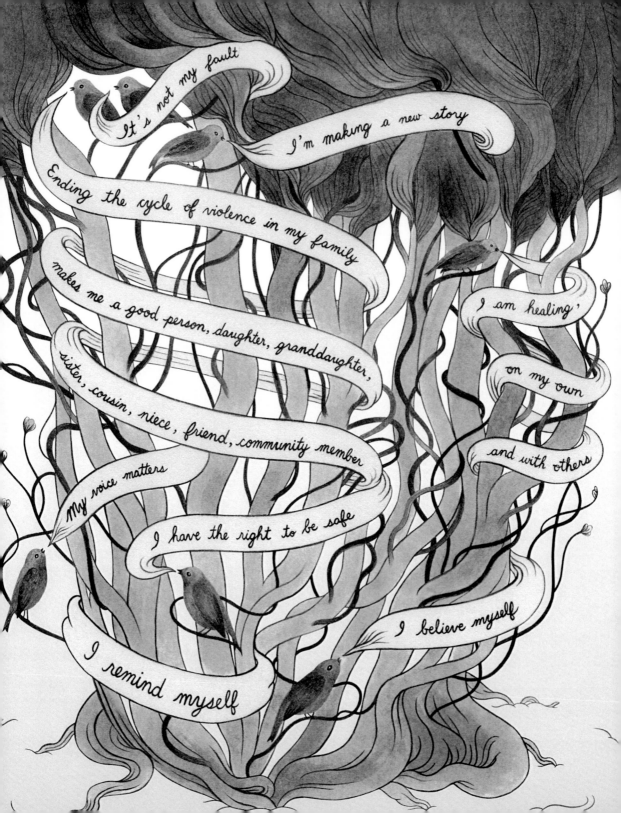

The Tree

I HEARD SETTLERS HAVE COME TO THIS AREA. THEY ARE PLANNING TO TAKE ALL THE GOOD THINGS FROM HERE AND TRANSFER THEM TO THE OPPOSITE END OF THE WORLD.

REALLY?! I AM SOOOOO SCARED. WHAT TO DO? OMG!

WRITTEN BY : DHRUBOK
DRAWN BY : SOMYA SINGH

YOU MIGHT BE OKAY. YOUR ROOTS ARE PRETTY STRONG AND WELL CONNECTED WITH THE EARTH. NO ONE CAN PULL YOU OUT EASILY.

LATER

NOOOOOO OOOOO!

GOODBYE MY DEAR FRIEND. I WISH I COULD SAVE YOU.

THANK YOU! PRAY FOR ME, THAT I WILL BE FINE OUT AT THE OPPOSITE END OF THE WORLD.

CANADA

AFTER AWHILE, THE POMEGRANATE FRUIT CRACKED OPEN NATURALLY WITHOUT ANY MANUAL TECHNIQUES.

SIGNS OF VIOLENCE

Does someone who says they love you (this could be anyone, including your immediate, extended family, faith group, peers)

Threaten to hurt you physically?

Isolate you?

Tell you stories about hurting someone because they disobeyed a community code of conduct?

Hack into your email or social media, monitor your phone, harass you at work or school, or other forms of stalking?

Threaten to or hurt people that are important to you i.e. partners or children?

Use their anger to intimidate or control you?

Threaten to hurt your pets?

Stop you from attending school, work, community events, or places of worship?

Kidnap you?

Force you to marry someone you do not want to?

Insult you, or put you down in public? In private?

Blame you for their own difficulties?

Threaten to kill themselves or others if you cross a boundary?

THAT'S NOT LOVE
    THAT IS ABUSE.

Dear Priyan,

WRITTEN BY : ANJALI - PRIYAN
DRAWN BY : SOMYA SINGH

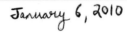

January 6, 2010

Dear Priyan,

Tonight was beautiful. The women at the centre are amazing — I feel welcomed. I realized, tonight, that I don't want to ignore you anymore. Please continue to show your compassion for me even in times when I have none for myself. You are my younger self and I love you.

I feel scared. I have changed alot; I feel closer to you now Priyan. I am taking control of my life.

This woman in GENDER STUDIES class shows me I can still have those feelings that have been buried for so long. My anger and hate are washed away when I am beside her...

continued ⟶

... I know I am dangerously different. I try to understand this difference every day, this difference is called **QUEER**. It gives me so much pride and confidence, but I am also scared. Fearful of hate. Sometimes I wish this didn't exist in me, but I know that denying it will take me further away from you Priyan! With so much compassion, beauty and courage,

Love ♡
Anjali

$A^2 + B^2 = C^2$

IN FIGHTING FOR THE LIVES OF MY PEOPLE I REGAINED MY VOICE AND A SENSE OF BELONGING I NEVER HAD.

SPRING 2010

HEALING IS A PROCESS...

KNIFE

The edge of the knife,
Against my arm.
Stabbing pain in my chest.
Breath caught.
Twisted inside of me.
Twisted breath and words
Burst out in tiny hiccups.
If you listen carefully,
you will hear voices
woven in tiny hiccups.
Priyan is speaking.
Breaking the silence.
She can't hide anymore.
She is too big to hide inside of me.

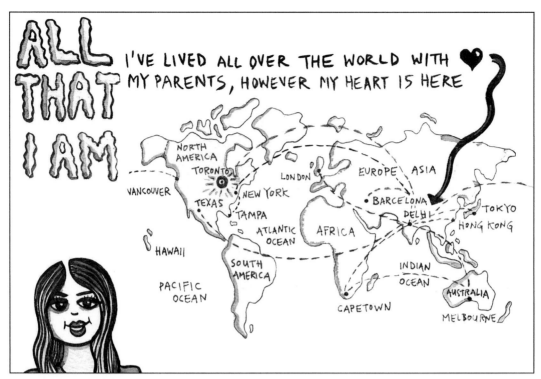

ALL THAT I AM

I'VE LIVED ALL OVER THE WORLD WITH ♥ MY PARENTS, HOWEVER MY HEART IS HERE

WRITTEN BY: KATHANA RATNAKARA
DRAWN BY: SOMYA SINGH

TORONTO

YOU'RE GOING TO BREAK IT OFF WITH RYAN...

AND YOU'RE COMING HOME IN 3 WEEKS...

I'LL GET YOU A JOB AT MY FRIENDS' BUSINESS...

NEW DELHI

Reputation

Health

Money

Honour

Career

Family

Marriage

WHEN HEALING FROM VIOLENCE

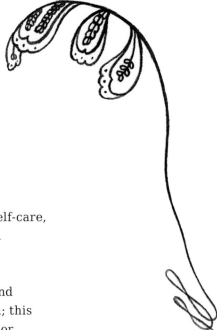

SEARCH
Look for books, movies, zines, stories, comics about healing, self-care, community care, trauma, abuse.

STRENGTHEN YOUR NETWORKS
Join groups or take a class around things that are important to you; this could be at a community centre or online, with artistic, recreational, cultural, or spiritual groups.

SAFETY PLAN
Expand the ways in which you stay safer; check out safety planning guides, or make your own with a friend or a counsellor.

SPEAK OUT
Talk to someone you trust. This could be a friend, a counsellor, an elder, a teacher, or a coach. They can listen to you or simply be present with you. They can also help you connect with resources and support.

SHARE
Remind yourself that you are not alone. Connect with your peers, build community, and reach out. This could be by attending a group for survivors of violence, creating social media about how you are feeling, or making art for yourself.

SELF-CARE
Set aside intentional time to nurture your spirit, mind, body, and heart. This could mean partaking in a spiritual practice of your choice, reading a fun book, eating yummy food, or sitting in a park.

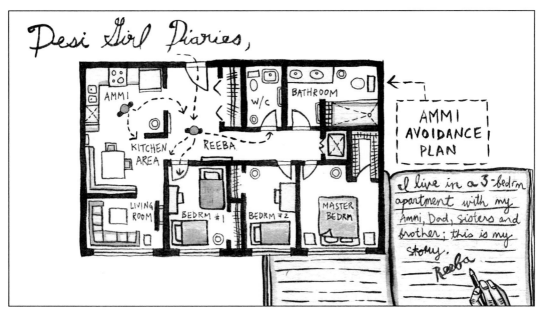

Desi Girl Diaries,

AMMI AVOIDANCE PLAN

AMMI · KITCHEN AREA · REEBA · W/C · BATHROOM · LIVING ROOM · BEDRM #1 · BEDRM #2 · MASTER BEDRM

I live in a 3-bedrm apartment with my Ammi, Dad, sisters and brother; this is my story.
—Reeba

WRITTEN BY : M. AFTAB
DRAWN BY : SOMYA SINGH

REEBA!!

WHERE HAVE YOU BEEN?! SCHOOL ENDED 3 HOURS AGO!!

WHAT IS THIS VOLUNTEERING NONSENSE?!! ALWAYS SURROUNDED BY NON-MAHRUM BOYS!

AMMI, I WAS VOLUNTEERING AFTER SCHOOL, REMEMBER I TOLD YOU ABOUT THE GRAFFITI PROJECT...

AND ALL THIS GRAFFITI RUBBISH! FOCUS ON SCIENCE AND MATH. YOU'RE GOING TO MEDICAL SCHOOL AND THAT'S FINAL. IF YOU WANT TO VOLUNTEER, GO WORK IN A HOSPITAL.

BUT AMMI, IT'S FOR A GOOD CAUSE! IT'S FOR RAISING AWARENESS ABOUT MENTAL ILLNESS IN OUR...

HOW DARE YOU RAISE YOUR VOICE!! BEYSHARAM! WHAT MENTAL ILLNESS?! WITH A DAUGHTER LIKE YOU, I WILL BE THE ONE TO GO CRAZY. SELFISH GIRL!! GET OUT OF MY SIGHT!

AT HOME

Dear Diary,   January 9th
I had no other choice...

SSSSHHHH

I feel awful that he's mad, but I can't do this. What if someone finds out?

EARLIER THAT MONTH

I CAN'T DO THIS ANYMORE, IT'S NOT RIGHT.

YOU'RE JOKING, RIGHT?

WE'RE TOO DIFFERENT. IT'S NOT GOING TO WORK OUT. TRUST ME.

WTF

REEBA, I CAN'T BELIEVE **THIS**! I THOUGHT YOU WERE DIFFERENT...

BUT YOU'RE JUST LIKE EVERY OTHER MANIPULATIVE **BITCH** OUT THERE!

HOW I HONOUR MY HEARTBEAT

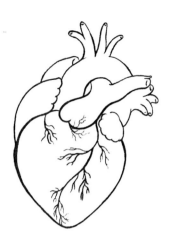

Caged

WRITTEN BY : MARIAM A.
DRAWN BY : SOMYA SINGH

I WONDER IF SAFIYA WILL COME TODAY? I CAN'T BELIEVE SHE LEFT HOME, IT'S SO WRONG. HOW COULD SHE DO THAT TO HER PARENTS?

HALA COULDN'T HELP BUT THINK WHAT IT WOULD BE LIKE TO LIVE OUTSIDE OF THIS COMFORTABLE, YET CONTROLLING NEST. WOULD SHE BE HAPPY? WOULD SHE MAKE IT ON HER OWN.

WHAT'S THE POINT IN DREAMING? MY PARENTS WON'T EVER APPROVE - THEY WATCH MY EVERY MOVE.

SAFIYA! YOU CAME! MY MOM TOLD ME NOT TO TALK TO YOU, THANKFULLY SHE'S OUT HUNTING FOR WORMS.

HOW'S THAT FAIR? YOUR PARENTS ARE MAKING YOU GET MARRIED YOU NEED TO GET OUT OF HERE!

MY PARENTS MAY BE STRICT, BUT THEY LOVE ME VERY MUCH. I CAN'T JUST TURN MY BACK ON THEM! THEY HAVE TAKEN CARE OF ME MY WHOLE LIFE. I AM NOT LIKE YOU!

OMG HALA!! DO YOU THINK THAT I'M TOTALLY SELFISH? THAT I JUST WOKE UP AND DECIDED TO LEAVE? DO YOU THINK IT WAS EASY?!!

NO, I...

DON'T YOU THINK I WISH THAT I COULD SEE MY MOM WITHOUT HAVING TO HEAR HOW BAD OF A DAUGHTER I AM? YOU KNOW MY DAD REFUSES TO EVEN SEE ME! NO MATTER WHAT HAPPENED, I LOVE THEM.

SAFIYA, I AM SORRY. I HAD NO IDEA, YOU NEVER TOLD ME. WHY DID YOU LEAVE IN THE FIRST PLACE?

SAFIYA: "I LEFT AT 16 'CAUSE MY MOM AND DAD WERE TRYING TO FORCE ME TO MARRY MY COUSIN JAVED. WHEN I TOLD THEM THAT I DIDN'T WANT TO, THEY SAID I DIDN'T HAVE A CHOICE."

"I TRIED TO TALK TO THEM, I PLEADED AND BEGGED, BUT THEY DIDN'T LISTEN. SO WHEN THEY ARRANGED THE ENGAGEMENT I COULDN'T GO THROUGH WITH IT. IT WASN'T FAIR TO JAVED OR ME."

MY PARENTS WERE ALWAYS CONTROLLING MY MOVEMENTS. I HAD A CURFEW, BUT MY BROTHER COULD FLY AROUND ANYTIME HE LIKED.

BUT ISN'T THAT THEIR RIGHT AS PARENTS?

Safiya's brother

WE ALL HAVE RIGHTS, HALA. YOU MUST GET OUT OF THERE. I'LL HELP YOU.

PECK

PECK

PECK

SUMMER

FALL

WINTER

SPRING | IN THE SPRING HALA BUILT UP THE NERVE TO MOVE OUT.

NO NO! Never. nooooo oooooo NO! NO Nah

WEDDING DATE

READY?

CLOTHES

I AM READY NOW.

I AM SO SELFISH...

CAN I LEAVE MY PARENTS?

WHAT ABOUT MOM? SHE'S GONNA CRY...

I HAVE TO DO THIS NOW! I KNOW I CAN, BUT I'M SCARED! I NEED TO DO THIS. I CAN TAKE CARE OF MYSELF. I AM LEAVING.

WHAT ABOUT MY HONOUR?

CONTRIBUTORS

ARUBA A. is a university student who is passionate about creating positive community change and supporting the self-empowerment of other young Muslim women.

FARRAH KHAN is a counselor, artist and educator committed to healing justice and transformative change.

KATHANA RATNAKARA is a writer and actress with great expectations.

M. AHMAD is an emerging artist specializing in photography, visual media, and fashion design. She believes that art is an invaluable and powerful form of expression and creativity when words alone are not enough.

NADIA ALAM is an artist. She sees things beautifully.

ROXANNA VAHED is an expressive arts therapist, theatre artist and community worker who is committed to transformative change and social justice.

SELENA WONG is a Toronto-based Illustrator who has a design degree from the Ontario College of Art & Design majoring in illustration. Her most recent accomplishments include winning a National Magazine Award in Gold for illustration.

S.B. is a chemist, aspiring freelance writer and philosopher.

SIVA is a Tamil-Hindu migrant from Germany who has lived on Turtle Island for about 22 years.

SOMYA SINGH BAS, M.Arch., MRAIC, OAA Intern is an Illustrator, Exhibition Designer and Intern, Architect. She is currently working on a comic that explores the historic partition of India and Pakistan and it's effect on South Asians living in present day Toronto.

ACKNOWLEDGMENTS

* Ancestors who dreamt that another world was possible and paved the way for us to speak out, we are eternally grateful * We honour those who fought/fight against the forces of colonization and patriarchy here on Turtle Island and beyond * Our elders, friends, community, family (biological & chosen), partners * Pomegranate Tree Group Advisory Committee: Mandeep Kaur Mucina, Suhail Abualsameed, Deepa Mattoo * Staff, Board & Volunteers at Barbra Schlifer Commemorative Clinic * Somya Singh * Selena Wong * Jamila-Khanom Allidina * Farrah Khan * Roxanna Vahed * Steve Phillips * Kashfia Rahman * Willow Dawson * Mariko Tamaki * Andrew Suri * Shahina Sayani * Aisha Wahid * Leah Lakshmi Piepzna-Samarasinha * Catherine Hernandez * Tahirih Justice Center * My strength Anisha, Janu, Ashley, Jessica and Lee * My parents, brothers and daughter and my true friends * Me, for ending the cycle of violence in my family * Allah, my parents and grandmother, my best friends, for being the amazing supporters that will always be there. Special thank you to T.N, F.A and S.M * My brother for being the greatest brother in the world, my Anthropology teacher who believed in me and taught me what school never did and my Nani Ama who travels with me in my heart * The IZZAT collective for their support and care * Courageous storytellers * you *

OUR PARTNERS

Forced Marriage Initiative

The Tahirih Justice Center is proud to partner with the Pomegranate Tree Group to present the U.S. publication of *Heartbeats: The IZZAT Project*.

The Tahirih Justice Center is a national non-profit organization that supports the courage of immigrant women and girls who refuse to be victims of violence. The Forced Marriage Initiative offers support to individuals regardless of age, race, class, gender, immigration status, nationality, sexual orientation, or religion. If you are facing or fleeing a forced marriage or know someone who is, contact the Forced Marriage Initiative at the Tahirih Justice Center. We can discuss your rights and your options, guide you through steps you can take to stay safe, and help you to find resources in your area, including emergency shelter, legal services, counseling, and other forms of help.

Phone: 571-282-6161
Email: FMI@tahirih.org
Website: www.preventforcedmarriage.org
        www.tahirih.org
Address: 6402 Arlington Blvd, Falls Church, VA 22042

OUR PARTNERS